SYSTEM DESIGN ACTIVITIES

FOCUSING ON THE ENTIRE SYSTEM

by

Ferreh Kamara

authorHOUSE®

AuthorHouse™
1663 Liberty Drive, Suite 200
Bloomington, IN 47403
www.authorhouse.com
Phone: 1-800-839-8640

First published by AuthorHouse 9/18/2007

ISBN: 978-1-4343-3433-6 (sc)

Printed in the United States of America
Bloomington, Indiana

This book is printed on acid-free paper.

ACKNOWLEDGMENTS

A lot of thanks goes to many instructors and faculties at Strayer University for being helpful to me throughout my learning; Towson University and Anne Arundel Community College as well. Special thanks go to my three children, Abu, Kayode, and Ussef, for being there and understanding. Thank God for giving me strength. This book is especially dedicated to my children, again thanks to all of whom I have not measured yet.

ABSTRACT

The research objective identifies the design activities of the systems development life cycle (SDLC). It provides an overview of the design components, specifying the way in which the system uses technology. The design of an effective information system requires integrating the major components in today's growing networking businesses that are involved during its life cycle. Many industries and government sectors are being impacted daily with inadequate or poor software design and hardware.

The focus for this research is based on the entire system, which identifies the application deployment and which then determines the architecture and the structure of the network. The application software identifies subsystems that relate to the network, database, and user-interface activities. The database, on the other hand, identifies the database and management-system types to be use throughout the process. Further, user interface specifies the way in which the inputs and outputs should be implemented, and its relation within the software and hardware.

TABLE OF CONTENTS

List of Abbreviations xi

List of Terms and Definition xii

CHAPTER 1
Introduction

Context of the Problem 2

Statement of the Problem..3

Research Questions and Sub-questions.......................4

Significance of the Study 4

Research Design and Methodology 5

Organization of the Study...6

CHAPTER 2
Literature Review System Design Activities

Designing and Integrating Networks..........................11

Designing the Application Architecture......................13

Designing the User Interface 15

Designing the System Interfaces 17

Designing and Integrating the Database 21

Prototypes for Designing Detail 23

Designing and Integrating the System Controls........27

CHAPTER 3
The Deployment Environment

Examining the Requirements and
Structures Bridged Within System.............................36

Single-Computer and Multi-tier Architecture............38

Centralized and Distributed Architecture 40

Computer Networks 41

The Internet, Intranets, and Extranets 44

CHAPTER 4
The Application Architecture

Client-Server Architecture 49

Three-Layer Client-Server Architecture 52

Middleware 55

The Internet and Web-based Application Architecture..............57

CHAPTER 5
Designing the Network

Network Integration...61

Network Description...63

Communication Protocols and Middleware 65

Network Capacity 68

CHAPTER 6
Summary and Conclusion

Introduction..72

Summary..73

Advantages/Disadvantages..74

Conclusion..76

The Future Trends of Systems Design 81

APPENDICES

Appendix A: Systems Design Survey Assessment 84

Appendix B: Project Coordination 87

Appendix C: The Three Tiers Tradeoffs...............................89

Appendix D: Application Communication Processing..............90

Bibliography..91

LIST OF TABLES

Table 1.0 Telecommunications network functions 41

Table 2.0 Intranet Benefits 45

Table 3.0 Network Benefits 51

Table 4.0 Middleware Layering 55

Table 5.0 Internet and Web-based benefits 57

Table 6.0 Internet and Web-based negativities..........................58

Table 7.0. The Types of Internet Connection.............................69

Table 8.0 Number of pages transfer..70

Table 9.0 Number of users handled...70

LIST OF FIGURES

Figure 1.0: Single, clustered, multi-computer. 38

Figure 2.0 Router connects networks..42

Figure 3.0 Routers interconnect four networks.........................43

Figure 4.0. Client-server architecture......................................50

Figure 5.0 The Three-Layer Client-Server 53

Figure 6.0 Firewall connects company's network 61

Figure 8.0 Synchronous or asynchronous 66

Figure 9.0 Connect-oriented 66

LIST OF ABBREVIATIONS

API - Application Programming Interfaces
CGIC - ommon Gateway Interfaces
CORBA - Common Object Request Broker Architecture
CSS - Cascading Style Sheets
DBMS - Database Management Systems
DCE - Distributed Computing Environment
DLL - Dynamic Link Libraries
EDI - Electronic Data Interchange
FDDI - Distributed Data Interface
HTML - Hypertext Markup Language
HTTP - Hypertext Transfer Protocol
IP - Internet Protocol
LAN - Local Area Network
OCR - Optical Character Recognition
ODBC - Open Database Connectivity
OO - Object-oriented
OS - Operating System
SDLC - Systems Development Life Cycle
SET - Secure Electronic Transaction
SOAP - Simple Object Access Protocol
SQL - Structured Query Language
TCP/IP - Transmission Control Protocol and Internet Protocol
VPN - Virtual Private Network
WAN - Wide Area Network
WWW - World Wide Web
XML - eXtensible Markup Language

LIST OF TERMS AND DEFINITION

Application architecture: application software that functions within system network.

Client/server architecture: is responsible for the process of application that separates the two programs into client and server.

Database Management Systems (DBMS): the process that ensures the data in the database is accurate and consistent, including data dictionary, data storage, data transformation, security, multi-user control, backup/recovery, integrity, language/application interfaces, and communication.

Database design: the process of designing the database structure that would house the data.

Deployment environment: the process that configures computer hardware, software, network, and standards.

E-commerce: the process of conducting businesses online.

Internet: a global public-access network that connects a network of computers.

Middleware: a set of applications that enables business services and users to interact with others over a network

Network: consists of computer hardware, network, and operating system.

Prototypes: enable a quick system development.

SDLC: design components and specifying the way in which the system uses technology.

System interfaces: are inputs or outputs that requires any people's involvement.

Systems design: the process that describes, organizes, as well as structures the hardware and software.

User interface: provides the graphics windows, dialog boxes, as well as mouse for interacting among system and users. (Satzinger et al., 2004)

CHAPTER 1

INTRODUCTION

Context of the Problem

Many organizations today rely on the computer and information technology to do business and operate effectively. As a result, computer system software design is increasing rapidly in order to keep up with the changing information technology. However, designing a system requires detailed work during the tasks that were specified by the system analysts (Meyer & Baber, 1997). The Standish Group estimated a cancellation of 30 percent of software projects, half caused by going over budget, 60 percent failed to support the organizations that initiated this project, and most are due to lateness (Selectbs, n.d).

Further, the systems design goal is designing an effective, reliable, and maintainable information system. The effectiveness of a system defines the requirements and meeting its goals. However, when a system is ineffective, then it is not usable by end users; only the ones that are used are acceptable. The information system is said to be reliable if the system is error-resistant, but if input data errors, process errors, hardware failure, and human mistakes occur, it could be very expensive and complex to fix if not detected early. A system reliability approach must plan for errors, and detect them as they occur, for corrections.

An information system is said to be maintainable, simple, flexible, and modifiable if it is capable of correcting errors in the system that might occur, and allows enhancement of the system to take advantage of rapidly changing technology (Shelly, Cashman, & Adamski, 1995).

STATEMENT OF THE PROBLEM

With systems design, the hardware and software are identified as the processes for the system, and their interrelations are also described. The critical part of designing a good system is its quality, which is done before the building process begins (Martin, Brown, DeHayes, Hoffer, & Perkins, 2002).

The design of an information software system is very difficult and complex to carry on. Unfortunately, systems developers have not yet designed a fully workable system to accommodate or solve problems with business functions. Moreover, all systems need to be modified and updated constantly for any changes that might occur. For example, some processes might have been left off that needed to be added, fixing errors, or the system requirements; then upgrading must be done to ensure the system's correctness. Though the cost to maintain the system is as high as original ones, early detection would eliminate most costs associated with modifying the system. A good systems design makes the development of a system easy, quicker to operate, and maintainable (Satzinger, Jackson, & Burd, 2004).

Research Questions and Sub-questions

The most important part of a good design, we must follow the design process approach system design, in any case. When designing and specifying an information system, we ask the question: What types of hardware, software, and network and inputs and outputs design process are required?

Below are sub-questions to the problem to answer:

1. Examining the requirements and structures bridged within the system?
2. The system design activities carry by the people and hardware?
3. The various part systems used to communicate among each other all over the organization?

Significance of the Study

The fundamental aspect of this study explained how systems design could help with optimizing scarce computing resources in applications or system performance constraints. Also, the hardware and software played an important role in determining the way in which an application performs and the resources "bottleneck" as well.

In addition, the performance of an information system is an integral part of good quality. In today's competitive world, a business organization tries to achieve their service goals by employing systems that perform better. Knowing that your system will perform effectively increases business performance. Moreover, this study is significant in the fact that companies with technological limits turn to systems design to satisfy their changing requirements for better services (bls.gov, n.d.).

Research Design and Methodology

This research design and method is based on quantitative factors. These include primary, secondary, and survey sources. The primary sources include computer software, Web pages, and so on, which provide a vast amount of information to carry on with the research. Surveys and questionnaires are also considered to be primary sources. Secondary sources are measures that were based on primary sources and make it much wider to access; also, sources from books through libraries, and so on.

Additionally, the research method also includes tertiary sources, which are material collected through schoolbooks, encyclopedias, newsletters, and more. With triangulation, the combination of primary and secondary sources provides some benefits to utilize different kinds of research methods.

The survey is organized in questionnaire fashion, with closed-ended answering allowing the participant to respond to a rating ranging from 0 (the lowest) to 5 (the highest). Narrowing the problem, the questions were based on how the system output and user interface react to the users, because this is the most critical part of designing an information system. There were ten questions (see Appendix A), and sixteen copies were distributed. Only three responded, which makes up the percentage of responders to be 19 percent.

Finally, all of this information has provided a way to utilize the systems design activities and the issues underplayed in designing an information system.

ORGANIZATION OF THE STUDY

The organization of each chapter is based on what will be discussed. The process includes the best way to design a good information system. The chapters are organized into six sections and appendices.

CHAPTER 1—Introduction: We will be discussing the context of the problem. Statement of the problem states the objectives for conducting the research. The research questions and sub-questions, on the other hand, are based on answering the research objectives.

In addition, we discuss the significance of this study, which has provided an understanding for conducting the research. Research design and methodology, the methods used for completing the research, are also discussed. Finally, the organization of the study of how each chapter is based.

CHAPTER 2—Literature Review: System Design Activities provides an overview of design activities which serve the construction of a new system. These include designing and integrating a network, the process where we specify all communication activities for an organization, designing the application architecture, designing the user interface, designing and integrating the database, design prototype details, and designing and integrating the system controls for safe-guide.

CHAPTER 3—The Deployment Environment involves specifying the hardware, software, and the network for the new system. It includes single-computer and multi-tier architecture, centralized and distributed computer networks, the Internet, intranet, and extranets. These all will be discussed in detail in the chapter.

CHAPTER 4—The Application Architecture. We discuss client-server architecture, three-layer client-server architecture, and the Internet and Web-based application architecture.

CHAPTER 5—Designing the Network. This includes network integration, network description, communication protocols and middleware, and network capacity.

CHAPTER 6—Summary and Conclusion. This chapter is more focused on concluding the design activities, advantages and disadvantages, and trends of design. Also, we look into the future of systems design. Finally, the research study includes some appendices that are discussed in detail as moving along with the study, which includes survey, and so on.

CHAPTER 2

LITERATURE REVIEW SYSTEM DESIGN ACTIVITIES

This review literature objectively examines the system design activities, which provides a view of the information technology and its issues. The systems design focuses on the construction for building of new information systems, which describe, organize, as well as structure the hardware and software. Systems design works like building a new car; all various parts must be specified and organized in order to build it. Fitting the different parts together is very complex, because each part must be compatible.

With design activities, as measured earlier, is the process that addressed the structuring, organizing, and describing in-depth of how the system would work into a different organizational setting (Satzinger et al., 2004). Though some of the design detail sometimes did along during the systems analysis and the system activities. The repetition process is usually employed during these activities. This is accomplished by one repetition after another until a solution is met.

In addition, most organizations that have information systems sometimes include many programs or in-house software packages. Systems analysts must try to adapt to their preferences and user tools. Promoting a good integration between the ever-changing user's needs and information systems methods, we must develop a system that would ensure these changes (Whitten, & Bentley, 1998). Moreover, the new system must be able to identify all of the information presented correctly, and provide integration between network systems. As within system documentations, that could be distributed to ensure integration or consistency (Satzinger et al., 2004).

Designing and Integrating Networks

When connecting with many computers, we form a network to share or exchange information that integrates others. The networks used today include local area network (LAN), which provides one area, and wide area network (WAN), which provides service for more than one area. There are applications that make it possible to provide network services, such as Internet protocol. This transmission control protocol and Internet protocol (TCP/IP) ensure guidance to the network in terms of data problems or others (Torres, M.J., Sideris, P., 2005).

The implementation of a new system is usually done with the new network; doing so would require the design of it as well. We will discuss network design and integration, along with the issues involved in chapter 5. A network consists of computer hardware, network, and operating system for the new system. Most information systems require installation to a network and client server (Satzinger et al., 2004). When designing a new system, you would include the configuration of a network platform. At times, the design of a network is already complete in terms of the existing system, but sometimes requires developing an operating system needed to satisfy the new system's levels of performance. The critical factors affecting the integration of a system with a network are reliability, security, throughput, and synchronization.

Moreover, the flowing of hardware improvements brings about the software, and then the application development and tools, which evolve on grounds. Client/server computing fits into a distributed environment. The systems are implemented as individual components, which makes them unique to the system. Client elements interact with users and servers that involve in many computing environments.

The clients and servers use hardware and software to suit the requirement functions of the system. The front-end and back-end systems that are sometimes used for computing have different type and power from each other. The database management systems are designed to handle queries, whereas the graphical functions part memory and computing, which create the displaying of graphics.

The benefit of installing client/server computing is that the hardware servers range from small uni-processors to large parallel ones that contain thousands of processors for communication. Many companies today are matching the capacity of their server to handle such processes. If, for some reason, the server stops working, the old server takes over. This in turn provides scalability, flexibility to the growing hardware, rather than centralized mainframe to reduce costly upgrades.

When designing and integrating a network, the data transfers between client and server must be minimized to prevent network traffic. Communication networks are very slow and open to errors in many systems where they are interconnected, resulting in poor performance due to such effects. A good design mapping between this data and processes would result in a better transfer of data. Planning ahead of time before placing the system into use is very important (Loosely, & Douglas 1998).

The information system strategic planning, called new or improved information systems, defines the technology and application to support an organizational plan. The top management plans for the entire organization to see what needs be to be addressed, which gives them an open door to consult or hire staff to complete the project plan. This staff then examines the locations of the business functions, creates, uses, and integrates the information systems, sometimes called application architecture plan (Satzinger et al., 2004).

In the next section, we are going to discuss the application architecture plan, to better understand how these pieces fit together.

DESIGNING THE APPLICATION ARCHITECTURE

During the application architecture design, the information system must be designed to fit the user's preferences; we will discuss more in chapter 4 about this topic. Application architecture is application software that functions within a system network. During the design of application software, the user and database are designed as well. The design of the application must meet today's business requirement functionalities. Designing the software programs requires the use of computer tools to understand the various parts involved. Also, we must specify the detailed processes that must be carried. As long as the process has been specified, the physical models are designed in terms of the development and deployment variation. For instance, a programming language such as Visual Basic could be different from COBOL.

Programs that are written for mainframes are not to be used for single programs, due to the complexity of the system. Online coding programs can only function for online proposes; some programs are meant for other activities to carry out periodically, as well as programs for backup/recovery. So the composition of the whole system programs are executed as a single program.

Using client/server architecture is different from centralized architecture, because the computing environment is distributed in most areas. Also, object-oriented technology create used differently from other; since most processes are done by people instead of computers, a design for that purpose is needed (Satzinger et al., 2004).

Many systems are being used by enterprises; designing a full-deploy application requires some flexibility for systems to work together along with the new one. In turn, the application would be supporting the rapidly changing technology. It is mandatory today to design a system that would integrate with others. So, the choice of an application architecture that lays out all the now-and-then features is very important (Jonker, 2005).

Electronic commerce infrastructure is the computer systems of an organization, and integrates among high-level software as well. Also, it enables companies to create commerce systems software. The tools used by such companies include payment, purchase, secure data, etc. for business activities. When two or more companies integrate, it allows them to share and/or exchange business information to stay competitive. The most fundamental aspect of developing e-commerce is that the layering software used over transmission control protocol and Internet protocol (TCP/IP) provides system controls. Integrating e-commerce hardware and software with other systems is critical. For example, Web servers, which require more layers to implement because of their complexity (Brown, 2004).

Meanwhile, the combination of applications with object-oriented, client/server, and Internet technologies makes for a big payoff. Benefiting from combing makes the business more flexible and available. In turn, IT staff would be able to better plan the application configuration by mixing mainframes, midrange, and desktop/laptops for meeting business competition. In addition, application and platform developers should be clear about what is underlying among middleware and applications, keeping in mind that the middleware layers could be impacted with performance and cost (Umar, 1997). Designing interface is the representation of contracted client and server applications. This usually defines the parameters and identification of unique addresses. In the next section, we discuss the designing user interface of the application that the developer must design in order to allow an interaction between computer and human.

DESIGNING THE USER INTERFACE

The users of computer systems need control and assessment when working with computer systems. Systems that might have many user interfaces are usually used by several users, for instance, library databases could use a few interfaces for different purposes. Computer systems only look at the user of a particular computer and then make some reaction. Designing user interface is mission critical, because users providing input to get a system output and learning process is very important (Wikipedia, n.d.).

An information system depends on user interface, which defines the interaction between the user and computer. User interface provides the graphics windows, dialog boxes, as well as mouse to interact with. In addition, the interface is made up of sound, video, and voice, which might be different from one user to another. So designing a user interface is critical, which system analysts must thoroughly develop (Satzinger et al., 2004). The design of the user interface involves the design of input and output.

Further, the input is used to record and enter data with issued instructions into the computer system. The selection of an appropriate input device that would be safe, effective, and efficient is very important. Choosing an input device that would carry out the instruction contributes to a usable system. In turn, the trade-offs for choosing the appropriate input device are among its features. Systems with two or more input devices like keyboard and mouse must be able to provide guidance, reassurance, information, as well as making users' error corrections. This information must be visualized as changes are made. With auditory, the system must provide an audio warning to inform the user that an error has occurred (Rogers, Sharp, Benyon, Holland & Carey, 1994).

The output device, on the other hand, is the conversion of input data from electronic, the part of the computer entered by a human, the output. The evolution of output devices, including graphical user interface and multi-window, is becoming widely used in laptop and pocket computers as well. Other output devices such as vision, moving picture, and sound are being used with the combination of hypermedia systems. Interface designers must be concerned with the health of the users. The physical health issues of concern are blindness, color-blindness, sight, and hearing being affected in many computer users. So, in designing an interface, the designer must consider the displaying coloration. As measured by researchers, the background resolution may create a greater impact on humans.

The user interface design creates the software by putting the user in the center, instead of the computer system. Known as the user-centered design process, this provides some consideration about users' preferences (Microsoft, n.d.). Usability is the process system functionalities; this makes sure that the system is easy to use. Still, this process of making the function with various users and preferences is difficult. The interface designer must ensure the workability of the interface design and the evaluation (Satzinger et al., 2004).

When designing interfaces, the input and output must be defined, whether for the system interface or the user interface. The system interface design requires very little human involvement. The processing of the inputs is done by scanners, electronics, and batch, which is processed by others. This is especially good when producing and compiling documents externally. A user interface, as stated earlier, requires human involvement at all times, since the interaction is based on the human and the computer to input data. With the Web, on the other hand, the customer makes direct contact with the system by surfing the through the Net. Developing interfaces for both the user and system requires different designs, since the systems are usually done separately from one another; a system interface discussion is next.

DESIGNING THE SYSTEM INTERFACES

Most system interface design details the entire system that companies use for a means of either electronic, hard copies, automated, or no user devices. System interfaces are inputs or outputs that require any people's involvement. The automated input devices for system interfaces include scanning, bar coding, and optical character recognition (OCR) for computer processing. When designing and analyzing the system interfaces, the systems analyst must consider the increase in integration and interconnection, which requires system interfaces for input, output, fast, efficient, and accurate, to care the growing digital age. With system interfaces, input and output is done in real time interactively with other systems. The electronic data interchange, as well as Web, usually integrates by processing messages. With electronic data interchange (EDI), processing the data is done electronically without human input (Satzinger et al., 2004).

However, formatting EDI's transactions is very difficult, due to transactions being distributed to different systems at the same time or different times, and with other companies. Also, it is very expensive in terms of setting up and maintaining the system. Meanwhile, it is fast and easy to process transactions manually. Moreover, hypertext markup language (HTML) is another means of communicating that is embedded among systems for text formatting. In addition, eXtensible markup language extends HTML, which is a recent system version interface for text among systems (Satzinger et al., 2004).

With Web servers, the interaction between servers and middleware requires integration of the two. These types of interaction depend on Web server interfaces the Web server required. Web interfaces Web server interfaces process that interact with Web servers and middleware to communicate, provided that this is done through exchanging request responding, as well as messaging with outside sources. The most commonly used Web server interfaces for networking are common gateway interfaces (CGI) and application programming interfaces (API) (Rob & Coronel, 2004). The common gateway interfaces (CGI) are the process that is used to specify any passing parameters that are in PERL, C++, etc., for retrieving Web documents using HTML. Unfortunetely, CGI files decrease the individual external execution of programs. This, in turn, slows the system's ability to perform efficiently. The application programming interface (API), a Web server interface, is the processing that took place during file sharing known as dynamic-link libraries (DLL).

Further, the design of system inputs is based on defining types of input devices that could be used, since there are many ways to enter data into the system. This should provide some interconnection among the application, user, and system interfaces for transmits. Systems controls, security, and policies, on the other hand, are the process that must be thoroughly defined when designing, whether user or system interfaces. The processing of large amounts of data could cause errors from an input source; these errors could be reduced by developing an application that reviews processes that enter the system. These errors might be caused by users' typos. Input devices used to prevent users from keying data include magnetic card strip, bar code, optical character recognition, scanner, touch screen, digital camera, and audio. These devices are used in almost every department store and other places (Satzinger et al., 2004). Digital signature is another method that is required by law to be used for capturing data digitally instead of using hard copy, and errors are reduced as well.

Although the process that reduces errors does not guarantee it to be 100 percent error-free, it eliminates as much as possible. So accessing the system by unauthorized users may not be allowed due to fraud. Identifying all detail design of system interfaces is a critical part of an information system. The detail design of the systems interfaces requires that the designer define every requirement specification.

Moreover, designing a system interface provides the overall systems specification output, application, controls, and prototype. The main objectives during this stage of output and application design is the evaluation of the models that were presented by the system analyst; this sometimes includes ad hoc reports. The systems controls are also included during the designing of the system outputs, for security purposes. There are tools available for the development of such outputs. The systems analyst must provide full specification and requirement of the new system outputs. Though, the user interface output design requires no human involvement, but also display output on screen or turnaround documents. With documentation reports, the design is very complex due to the amount of information and the representation.

The outputs report consists of detailed, summary, exception, and executive reports that systems analysts should design for organizational use. Detailed reports are used by low-level management for accounting purposes, such as daily transaction and overdue account collection. Summary reports are used daily or monthly by middle-level management for account information. Exception reports provides the monitoring of the performance of an organization's reports summary. This report could be examined daily or weekly for record-keeping. High-level management, to evaluate the company's overall performance, uses executive reports. Moreover, internal and external outputs are also considered during the design processes. Internal outputs consist of organizational reports. External reports are those reports an organization must produce for another company, such as payment notification. The electronic reports are link reports that provide an organization's display reports in relation with information needed. The benefit of using hyperlink display is that it allows users to change reports at any time as needed. With electronic reports, users can combine or view reports from different areas for comparing with others, as well as graphics and multimedia (Satzinger et al., 2004).

The processing reports designer ensures that all detail reports specifications are identified. Designing reports is complex because of the large amount of information presented during design. Focusing on what is needed to be on the report is important, and the designer would find it easy to understand the processes (Satzinger et al., 2004). The interface "bottlenecks" are usually not easy to recognize; it takes some time to know exactly what it is going with the system. The problems could result from inefficient processing that might sometimes be due to information overload. In order to get a better understanding of the interface scales is to minimize data load (CMS Watch, n.d.). When designing system interfaces, the designer needs to specify the types of output devices and transmission bandwidth that will be used for scalability, efficiency, flexibility, user-friendliness, and maintainability. This system requires a thorough technical background to design the interface system. The database design is also a system design activity for modeling data and issues, which we will discuss in the next section (Satzinger et al., 2004).

Designing and Integrating the Database

The design of a database is crucial; database designers must take a good care how the data is represented. Database design is process of designing the database structure that would house the data, instead of database management systems (DBMS). DBMS is a process that makes sure the data in the database is accurate and consistent, including data dictionary, data storage, data transformation, security, multi-user control, backup/recovery, integrity, language/application interfaces, and communication.

The data dictionary or metadata is the process that looks up data in the database by the use of DBMS software. In addition, the data dictionary records alteration data in the database, in turn requiring no modification. Data storage management is responsible for storing and managing the data in the database, entity, screen, reports, rules, codes, format, and so on. It creates a turning test for storage and speed efficiency. Data transformation and presentation is for keeping the data independent structure for storage purposes. With data independency, DBMS is responsible for translating the data from logical to physical, for easy retrieval. The DBMS applications software is independent and represented in the same way. Security management secures user data and data privacy. In order to access data in the database, security ensures that the database is accessed by authorized users. Multi-user access, DBMS structures multi-users for accessing the database concurrently with control. The back and recovery management is used to save and/ or recover data in the database in case of systems malfunction, which is a crucial part of the database. With data integrity, DBMS minimizes data redundancy, maximizing data accuracy. The data access languages and application interfaces are query languages that are used within the database for data extraction (Rob et al., 2004). GUI tools are used to visualize data and business operations, to interact with data in the database. Application programming interface (API) is an application that lets programmers use their coding instead of rewriting new ones (Elmasri & Navathe, 2000). Database communication interfaces, on the other hand, is the communication design interface that allows users to communicate among interconnected computers. The designer must develop and gather information for viewing to specify the database. By observing the current system of the end user, the designer must then figure out how the data will be presented in the database. With systems interfaces, the designer must develop a mapping database to ensure accuracy. The accuracy of developing a model depends on the company, in which way their database should be represented. Still, they must have a good background multi-business to design one. Business rules are also part of an effective good design a designer must follow, which is critical to company procedures.

Database design that is either centralized or single-user, the requirement from distributed and multi-user databases is not the same. Moreover, hybrid object-relational database design is a combination of object and relational databases to stored objects. The design of a hybrid database is very complex because of various combinations of both. In distributed databases, which we will discuss more in chapter 3, the data is stored in different databases. In turn, a single process connects to various networks to do business (Rob et al., 2004). Distributed database design is the process that uses the breaking of database, logically known as fragmentation, as storage. The replication of data is also used to store data over many sites and allocations. The relationship that subset the tuples is stored horizontally as more attributes are specified. The vertical fragment relations are divided into columns from each site, keeping only the needed attributes. Mixed hybrid fragments combine many fragments to yield mixed. For instance, horizontal and vertical fragments, when combined each relation, they become mixed fragments. The replicating and allocating of data improves the data quality within a distributed database (Elmasri et al., 2000). The Web is an interconnection of networks that is a distributed database. The services that are included within the Web are news, messages, e-mail, FTP, e-commerce, and so on. Also, we can link information through link processing integration with several others. The users can browse or retrieve as much information as he or she can (Date, 2003).

The Web changes the way we do business, either by buying or selling goods through the Internet. Online databases shared among many others are complex to design; companies use information technology to conduct business. E-commerce database design requires the tools and a knowledgeable designer to build the database. The database should be able to link via the Web; it must be built for customer/product to minimize any problems that arise in the future.

Good database design generates better data management and valued output. When a database design goes wrong, it is usually caused by redundancy or duplication of data. As a result of data redundancy, the error-filled data becomes hard to locate. For instance, social security numbers for customers, agent files, invoices all stored together makes it hard for that particular customer (Rob et al., 2004).

Though a database is designed to handle sharing data within applications and systems, the complex database has jet perfect. The redundant data is being reduced and controlled among databases. The database's benefit is to store formatting data, since a database is separate in terms of information systems. The application programs specify which data should be in the end user's areas. In a database, independent data must be carrying at all times for consistency. Acing report and query can be achieved by various well-designed databases. Designing a database is very expensive, investing in the technology required. The designing methodology and tooling for databases provides some significant improvement (Whitten et al., 1998).

In addition, the database prototypes are created after the database schema for faster design. Since many DBMSs generate data definition language (DDL), this in turn creates prototype databases with DDL. This process is good in terms of performing prototype and test outputs, input screens, and components which result in quicker processing. In the next section, we will be discussing designing prototypes detail.

Prototypes for Designing Detail

Designing a quick prototype is necessary, one that could be used as a workable new system when they are built correctly. A working prototype would make all necessary operations processes work smoothly. Today's business and information technology changes; developing a quick and deploying information system for the implementation of the latest changes is crucial to be successful. The tools that are available now provide a short way to implement such systems. Since system users expect their systems to function as current changes emerge, a prototype enables a quick system development. These systems are sometimes built half-done or close to new systems requirements. More discovery and developmental systems are mostly used prototypes. The discovery prototype is rapidly used to analyze the new system requirements in systems design. The developmental, the processes are usually kept as the new workable system, also to develop an iterative software. The developmental approaches can be combined with either traditional or object-oriented (OO) if they are the same. The designing and implementing is different from conventional design. To design and implement parameters is done from top-down, which requires that these parameters be divided into subdivisions. After parameters have been specified, the detail requirement for developing a prototype is determined.

Prototyping is a means of developing a quick, fast system so that users can provide some examination of the system. A complete verification of the system is done with a prototype. Further, the success of a prototype system depends on the architecture and being feasible. Programs that are not communicating with each other can cause a problem during testing. These programs can be formulated using a conventional or object-oriented approach.

Prototype tools provide systems designers a way to develop a flexible and efficient system design. Such tools include Microsoft Visual Studio .NET, Oracle, as well as PowerBuilder for design satisfaction. The most fundamental aspect of developing a prototype is its speed, and accurately defining the user requirements. Constructing and modifying the system, the tools make it possible to so without spending a lot of time. A prototype that is powerful and flexible requires the development to be interactive. The process of developing a user interface prototype creates a way in which user can interact within the system. All tools perform a different function from each other, like database management systems and Web site and so on. Choosing the right tools is critical in terms of suitable deployment, implementation, and interfaces. Most tools today are used in designing software to intercommunicate with one another. Some software packages are also used for designing software. The software that interoperates with each other includes object-oriented, component-based, and Web.

Component-based software is an interoperable ready-to-use that requires standardization development. For instance, grouping computer and video shows that the two are compatible. Interoperation through one hardware is difficult, since components are distributed Web protocol are needed to fulfill this requirement. In the implementation of components, a designer must understand the systems requirements in detail application, communicate, and capably configure the system (Satzinger et al., 2004).

Moreover, designing a user-centered is based on the Internet that requires different types of standardization, programs as well as HTML, XHTML, and relational databases to control the information (Lash, 2003). The graphical design objective is to manage the way users do their computing, especially through the Web, in turn allowing them to gain the ability to use the Internet (Webstyleguide, n.d.). With cascading style sheets (CSS) tools, the user-centered is designed with a prototype. When CSS combines hypertext markup language and eXtendible hypertext markup language, creating user-centered prototypes is faster, and easy to design. CCS provides ways to allowing easy, faster download of information, among other things. The benefits of CSS provide a way in which an organization should concentrate on modeling processes, enable faster interactivity, and testing various processes. HTML is responsible for modeling sites; an application hierarchy is broken into small components, ensuring that the information is properly stored.

The process of linking pages requires XHTML, then provides an easy way to define the issues underling the system. CSS with XHTML makes a quick design process for prototyping, and applies the site in question. Many CSS have the ability to generate multiple designing processes. Also, data tests usually help with the identification any issues or errors that occur. The use of CSS can reduce the amount of time required to develop a prototype. XML can store data by using rapid prototype, data-driven, and query to the designing procedures. The Web standardization has provided a means of accessing the Internet, from conducting a business to educational purposes. Keep in mind that the user-centered process would be currently designed (Lash, 2003).

In addition, another interactive development approach known as spiral is used to develop software applications and prototypes as well. In the spiral approach, the first thing to do during the process is gather information to initiate prototyping. Spiral requires less information detailing design, whereas in prototype, more detail is required. The prototyping tools reduce the developmental time to produce a workable system. Developing spiral presents some pros and cons, including high parallel, that is programs overlapping each other. User involvement is required for the identification of systems requirements. Resource commitment ensures that the requirement is being utilized properly. The delivery, on the other hand, ensures the system is working and tests are conducted to improve flexibility.

Spiral development is a complex procedure that makes the design process very crucial. The systems analysts must understand the interdependency between functionality, life expectation, and experience. When a system is in higher independence, it creates design problems that might affect the system's ability to function. The life of any system should be four years or less, resulting in a better system modification (Satzinger et al., 2004).

Designing and Integrating the System Controls

The designing and integrating of the system controls ensures that the system is safeguarded from intruders. System designers must design integrity and security controls, due to various inputs and outputs. This open access forces one to rethink the effectiveness of security controls. The networks are built to allow many different accesses from internal to external entities. The designing of these controls prevents many mistakes or hackers from accessing the system. The integrity controls make sure that any data coming in or out is valid. To maintain this validation, the Internet makes some walkthrough. Many companies are concerned about this issue of Internet connectivity security, especially electronic markets and sales.

The design of integrity controls an information system's secured information within the system. Connecting to the Internet for companies that allow their workers, customers, and suppliers requires some security and integration of the system. Developing an application and database integration is crucial to success of the company; this is known as integrity controls. When the operation system and network are controlled, this is known as security controls, which we will discuss in detail later.

Developers must try to design integrity controls mainly for the internal access that a company might be having problems with. The main objectives are to ensure that any information obtained is not tampered with, transactions are properly handled, and to secure the hardware, software, and data, ensuring the information is not tampered with by unauthorized outsiders. This ensures that transactions are properly handled, meaning error-free, and with fraud detection by alerting users of any problems that might be occurring during data processing. The security of hardware, software, and data should address any malfunction. The protection of computer data, employees, and hackers is very important. In order to make sure that the information is entered correctly, we must design input integrity controls.

The electrical devices responsible for input data, known as a keyboard, prevent errors from entering the system, but do not guarantee it to be error free. It is said that what you put in is what you get (WYPWYG). The objective is to minimize errors from entering the system. A batch first processing input style known as keypunch allows a person to key data and another person verify the process. Today, many forms of input technique devices are available. The field combination controls review data for correctness, for instance, with applications for student enrollment for classes, when dates must be the same as the actual registered classes. Value limit controls must ensure that any numbers entering the system are correct, and no more than required. In other words, the system must be able to handle such numbers. With completeness controls, the data must be complete. For instance, any original data entered into the system in the past must be complete by entering all necessary information. The data validation controls make sure that numbers are entered correctly. Check-digits are usually used to calculate any previously entered data, to prevent any errors. Designers must design systems to prevent such controls in the system from occurring.

When designing database integrity controls, the DBMS includes access control, encryption, transaction control, update, and backup and recovery. In accessing, a user can gain access to the system, because the system security provides access. In database, the controls are thought of as interrelated data. For example, name, social security number, and salary are referenced as employee table. DBMS provides security that would verify the user during system accesses. The implementation of security controls could be different from one another, depending on the type of system used. The data encryption is a process that databases and data transmitters use to encrypt data from the outsider. In other words, the data is not readable by another person other than its intended. The transaction controls, the database requires logging into the system with proper user identification to prevent errors from entering the system. This DBMS software prevents systems fraud and denied access to the system. With update controls, process that update records within the system. The supporting software allows application programs to provide access/update simultaneously. The backup and recovery control is the process of protecting databases during system malfunctions and hackers. The backing up of data, whether half or full, must provide a copy of all system files recovered. In other words, the data are duplicated and kept at a different location.

Systems output, other than internal reports, screens display subjects to output integrity controls. Output integrity makes sure that any output coming from outside sources is properly transmitted to its destination. The destination controls handle processes that are needed to distribute it to its proper place. The routing of information to each location requires that information is in a printed fashion. The electronic outputs, whether online or batch, require particular destination controls. The integration of these systems is required for information exchange consistency. Acknowledgment among data network transmission is crucial. Designers must be able to distinguish among network and operating systems capabilities. The identification of such capabilities ensures that the system can work together to better distribute information over the Web. Controlling output files, whether in tape or disk, etc., the data entered must be correct. Screen outputs, on the other hand, are printed reports that many people use today. Designing output integrity controls, designers must carefully describe how the program fits together. Complete, accurate, and correct controls are inside processes that the system designers use to ensure that the design is done properly. The output print consists of date and time, date and time reported, time period, headers and description, routed information, page numbers, totals and footnotes, trailing, and version number and date (Satzinger et al., 2004).

The fraudulent integrity controls are designed to control fraud from reoccurring. Though the systems are not yet proven to be effective. System analysts must work with users to see whether the problems can be prevented. Each year, millions of fraud-related cases around the globe are being reported, due to inadequate fraud controls. Designers must design a system that would eliminate fraud.

When designing security controls, the primary goal is to design a system that would prevent intruders from accessing the system; the same applies to integrity control. In maintaining a stabilized system thereby protecting organizational a free of outside such as intruders, loaded information, worms, and viruses. Since many companies rely on the Web, any information transmitted is open to many various attacks. Securing the operating system would mean to eliminate or control what could interrupt the systems environment. In addition, protecting batch processing over the Net is another concern because of the sending and receiving of information from either customers or suppliers. As long as this valuable information is transmitted, it could be subject to interruption and modification. The safeguard mechanisms would prevent this information from being tampered with.

These safeguard mechanisms can be used with network or DBMS; because the network and operating environment are mostly used, securing the system is enforced. Companies' file management systems and end users are the most vulnerable ones to think of when securing the system. The system designers must design security controls that would distinguish authorized and unauthorized users before the data storage. Though designing and implementing security controls are very complex to do, it must be done in order to protect a company's assets.

When securing for access to a system, implementing security controls is required for Web, operating systems, software, hardware, data, applications, and network. Securing such systems would eliminate improper entries, because its functionality is embedded within the system. In turn, the benefits are that it secures the hardware and Web within systems by providing controlled access. The disadvantages are that it requires IT staff, especially the application implementation. The operating system (OS) and Web designers knew that designing or implementing such controls is complex and costly. Therefore, they must embed this software within. They also must distinguish different users when designing and implementing the system controls, consisting of registered, unauthorized, and privileged users.

The people who are not given the opportunity to access the system are called unauthorized users, such as employees, former employees, hackers, and/or intruders. The designer of the systems must be able to design security controls that could verify these activities. Registered users, on the other hand, are given the authority for the viewing or updating of information. These various accesses should be specified before the system is ready for the end users. Authorized users are those the system recognized, who have full access to the system. The access control list, many information seekers are able to or authorized during resource navigation. Moreover, privileged users are analysts or system designers to view or modify source code, programs, or the structure of the database. The system programmers, application operators, administrators, or others are usually given the privilege to access some degree for such systems (Satzinger et al., 2004).

Additional authentication, accessing database, Web, or online transactions allows people to access the system with proper identification. Especially when using a local area network (LAN) usually connects many users within. For instance, a person with an assigned user ID and password could easily be granted access (Rob et al., 2004). Creating a password is one thing to remember the pass code. The design of the security pass code is supposed to be different from one another, to permit access to systems. In that case, it is hard to remember all of the different IDs or pass codes at the same time.

Smart card is a read card that stores very little secure information; only a scan device can read it, as in debit or credit cards. This is encrypted data created for pass codes, fingerprints, retinal scan, and voice recognition. To verify a user, the card simply uses the scanning device to identify the user. It also provides security to limit hackers from accessing the system. In biometric devices, authentication is based on personal information such as keystroke, fingerprints, retina, or voice. The end-user keystroke, the system identifies the way in which the keys are being selected, the time it took, and forces. Other secure systems use this method to allow access and avoid any illegal entries. Biometrics has been used today by various organizations. The underlying thing about biometrics is that a human being becomes a pass code, which is usually built into hardware. The logical complexity of the system are patterns matching also programmed between mouse, keyboard, camera for monitor, or touch screens. In addition, the human iris or face can be use for scanning, enhanced by biometric devices. Biometric devices also provide different ways of entering the system. The levels where programs allow access are active for proper authorization. System designers must take a careful look with the different attributes presented and design what's appropriate (Satzinger et al., 2004).

In e-commerce, on the other hand, authentication permits users who conduct business online. In other words, customers placing an order or dealing with suppliers can easily change or modify transactions online without human intervention, as long as they are recognized by the system. Even though Internet authentication is complex, digital certificates usually allow customers or suppliers to access the system as well as credit card verification. With digital certificates and encryption combined, these mechanisms are capable of securing or authenticating users or data.

Encryption is the processing of coded versions using HTML styles, which are also acceptable with other applications or integrated. The e-commerce process requires security socket and hypertext transaction protocol to connect faster during transaction processing. The good thing about using security socket is that it secures a wide variety of accesses. The security of resource is the process of protecting the insider and outsider of an organization, preventing unauthorized users from entering the system. Firewalls or internal security protects organizational information from external misuse, as well as hardware and software.

Conducting business online, especially buying and selling, requires some forms of payment, such as credit card, digital cash, or wallets. The digital cash or currency identifies the person who is using it and must have a bank account in order to allow the transfer of funds between the purchaser's account and the payee. The advantages of using digital cash eliminates the cost of checkbooks used to pay for transactions. Transaction processing using digital cash is an expensive method; is hard to make changes due to business policies. Customers may prefer a credit card rather than digital cash. Another method, PayPal, is either by credit card or bank account through the Internet, secures and processes payments. This service is the most widely use today in more than thirty-five countries.

Processing credit cards on the Web is used as a form of payment manually with the use of secured Internet connectivity. There is a variety software available for manual processing systems which the bank uses to verify a customer's credit information. The customer, in turn, receives confirmed payment on a purchased item. The companies that issued the credit card, such as Visa or MasterCard, use a secure system known as secure electronic transaction (SET) in the process of securing the privacy of credit data via digital certificates, digital signatures, public-key during transmission, securing the communication among customer, supplier, and bank resources.

The advantage of SET is that it creates a quicker or faster credit information encryption. This method is the most preferred by many organizations or vendors like Netscape, Microsoft, IBM, or GTE. Moreover, SET specifies network and security required by company uses online pay identification. The internal firewall, encryption, digital signatures, encrypted database data, antivirus, operating system, authentication for users, auditing, and so on. The wallet is a form of payment that uses either credit card, digital cash, address, telephone numbers, or electronic mail, all considered to be physical. In this case, the electronic wallet programs are embedded within for auto purchase processing. Even though the electronic methods described provide some good news about doing business online, there are also systems design issues and concerns about security and privacy over the Internet (Rob et al., 2004).

CHAPTER 3

THE DEPLOYMENT

ENVIRONMENT

EXAMINING THE REQUIREMENTS AND STRUCTURES BRIDGED WITHIN SYSTEM

The most fundamental part of developing an information system is the deployment environment—how the hardware, software, network, and standard requirement fit together. Deployment environment is the process that configures computer hardware, software, network, and standards for the new application operation. Importantly, the deployment environment must work well with the application required for the new system. The systems analyst must specify in detail the computing alternatives for the design process. With the hardware, software, and network; the applications and deployment environment where one then, which was batch running on centralized. The files were stored on disk and tape without connecting to the Internet, with only keypunch as the source of data entry. Years passed by, and the technology changed the way computing is done. Many applications are being used today, such as software packages on mini or personal computers, distributed, Web-based, and others (Satzinger et al., 2004).

These applications are being supported by a variety of hardware, software, and networks. The sizes of hardware used today range from small to larger computers. Moreover, system analysts must choose the type of operating systems such as UNIX or Windows, DBMS as Oracle or DB2, infrastructure or standards as CORBA or .NET, or Web server as Internet Information Server or Apache. In order for the system's operation to go smoothly today, the software, network, and standard must be supported client and server hardware. The deployment environment requirement must include the following characters:

> The system required compatibilities
> The hardware and system software compatibilities
> The interface requirements for outside system
> The conformities within IT strategic and architecture plan

The system required that the user locations, speed, or update, security, and transaction processing signify the environment. For instance, the level of transactions processed per day or more including credit card payment-processing systems would need a secured high-speed Internet, server, operating systems, and database management systems that would be compatible among each other. Hardware and systems software compatibility are based on how technology has changed. In other words, when Oracle and Sun systems merge, any system changes occurring between the two would still integrate among each other. In addition, Microsoft operating and DBMS are integrated with processors such as Intel.

The most important thing to make sure about is that the hardware and software are compatible, to reduce high expenses. The systems external interfaces requirements bases on the outside processing such as credit agencies, customers, suppliers, or government. The requirements of some software must be specified, as well as hardware, because a credit reporting agency might use a Web-based XML to service their customers, or CORBA-compliant. The applications interaction among interfaces must be compatible with system software. Conformities within IT strategic and architectural plan, since the alternatives of software and hardware vary, companies are having problems finding a system that would integrate and cost as well. So companies with IT strategic and architecture try to reduce the way they plan for their purchases or setups. System costs and schedules, putting a project together for the deployment, the cost and schedule (see Appendix B for project coordination) depend on what is to be implemented. System analysts must specify the type of deployment that matches the application requirements.

SINGLE-COMPUTER AND MULTI-TIER ARCHITECTURE

The single computer, such as IBM S/390 G5 listed in Figure A, is the one that is usually attached to peripherals. Also, software packages for personal computers use a single computer as well. This is mainly recommended for much larger frames, because it allows user interaction. Due to the limited systems functions, the users must be at the same location. With single architecture, it is simply easy to do the designing, building, operating, maintainability of the system deployment (Satzinger et al., 2004). The downside of deploying a single computer with companies that consist of bigger information systems could create problems due to systems functionality. Some mainframe systems find it hard to process, store data, or retrieve information. This is where multi-tier architecture plays an important role in meeting required processes.

IBM S/390 G5

Figure 1.0: Single, clustered, multi-computer.

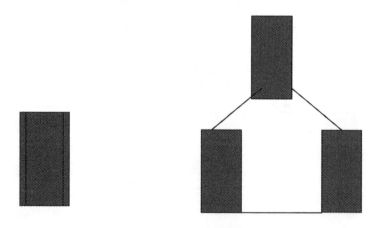

A. Single-Computer Architecture   B. Clustered Architecture

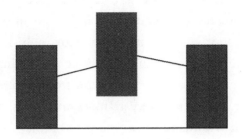

C. Multi-computer Architecture

The clustered architecture in Figure B consists of many computers that are connected to each other. This, in turn, helps the processing capacity, and the program execution remains at the same levels. With clustered connection, the system is considered single. The communication link is connected close to each other. The multi-computer architecture in Figure C, on the other hand, connects many computers. The clustered architecture requires that the operating system and hardware to be the same, however with multi-computer, the two can be dissimilar. Since the programs and data are in every system, each is designed to handle such processes.

CENTRALIZED AND DISTRIBUTED ARCHITECTURE

When centralized architecture resources are clustered, it means their central processing environment is located in one location. The centralized location allows data entry, with multi-locations within a company. Companies best suited for such processing include banks, insurance, or catalog sales entering data from different locations for that particular company. Every transaction that is processed can be batched; in other words the process can be offline.

The online entries central, such as order takers, can interact with many people. Transaction processing can be done over the Internet such as business-to-business. However, centralized architecture hardly uses platforms for information systems because of different processes that occur. Other systems can handle most transaction in real time. The implementation of the system requires one or more subsystems (Satzinger et al., 2004). Whenever data enters the system from a different location, it is known as distributed. The processing power is less expensive for personal and mini computers, increases the centralized processing, in turn boosting the distributed processing.

The distributed processing occurs in multi-locations where computers are connected via a communication network. The network consists of interrelated terminals, computers, and others for data sharing or LAN or WAN. Using both distributed and networks, it increases the power of information processing (Shelly et al., 1995).

COMPUTER NETWORKS

The computer networking allows an understanding of the relationship among hardware, software, and telecommunication, for role it plays within companies. Since such devices affect the way organizations do business, the need to know how they work and relate is important. The networking linked geo-distance devices for information sharing and/or data. With telecommunications, the communications are provided through distance with voice or data. When processes are done by telephone, the computer is doing process through distance via telecommunications from data origination. However, a network requires links between telephone lines. The core functions of a telecommunications network are listed in Table 1.0.

Table 1.0 Telecommunications network functions

Functions	What they do
Transmitting process	The network or and other responsible moving data or voice
The process	Making sure data or voice transmission OK
Edition	The information is correct and as well as formation
Convert	Changes codes
Route	Routes information efficiently
Network-control	Tracks communications status
Interface	Handles communication among users or network.

The transmitting data or voice requires the use of network or mediation. In order to move information, the process makes the correctness of its right place without mistakes. The edition checks for error-free or formats that might be out of order. Converting information is important, due to the movement of packages, especially WAN. The route of information provides an efficient way to process data. Network control, such as those measured above, keep of communication channels. The interface is a process that ensures interaction among users, and that the network goes smoothly (Martin et al., 2002).

The computer network consists of a local area network (LAN) and wide area network (WAN). LAN uses a single building to connect computers, where WAN can connect computers in cities around the world (Satzinger et al., 2004). However, the physical connection of the different networks is through a router. Routers are like bridges; a router can interconnect networks, also process and memorize and provide input and output interfaces for whichever connection is required (Comer, 2001). Router connections can either be two LANs, one LAN and one WAN, or two WANs. Figure 2.0 demonstrates such connections. Moreover, the connections more networks of the same functions, any technology used can different between networks. Today's computing requires systems integration. For instance, a router that is connected to an Ethernet LAN and FDDI LAN are not the same, but provide a communication link.

<u>NetworkRouterNetwork</u>

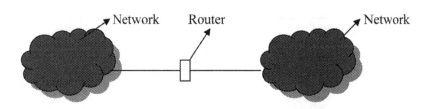

Figure 2.0 Router connects networks

In addition, organizations can use a technology that is most appropriate for their network needs in one connection. A router, mentioned earlier, can connect two more networks as a single Internet. Connecting all networks into more than three routers is the most efficient since the CPU and memory network traffic. Internet redundancy is reduced by using protocol software that manages the connections. To design such systems must be reliable, capable, and cheap to implement. Figure 3.0 illustrates how three routers connect LAN or WAN.

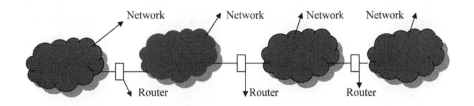

Figure 3.0 Routers interconnect four networks

The Internet, Intranets, and Extranets

The Internet is a global public access network that connects networks of computers for data transmission with the use of switches network Internet protocol (IP). The networks, such as a geographic area, schools, business, or government share information, including e-mail, chatting, files, Web pages, and others. To contrast the Internet and World Wide Web (WWW), the Internet is collection of computer networks connected linking through copper wires, fiber-optic, wireless, etc. The Web, on the other hand, are documents linked through hyperlink/URL to access the Internet. Wikipedia writers said the Internet will be use by more than 1.04 billion users, as of June 30, 2006 (Wikipedia b, n.d.). The Internet protocols standard, makes it possible to establish communication as follows.

➢To format or link data includes hypertext markup language (HTML), eXtensible markup language (XML), and hypertext transfer protocol (HTTP)

➢To execute programs, includes Java, JavaScript, or Visual Basic Script (VBScript)

➢In order to distribute software or services includes distributed computing environment (DCE), common object request broker architecture (CORBA), or simple object access protocol (SOAP)

The Internet infrastructure itself is based on a Web that provides services to end users (Satzinger et al., 2004). The Internet suites depend on the media devices that carried the information. So, any application protocols must be specified, because some applications are used only for specific purposes, as in the commercial or private sector. The WWW provides search engines such as Google to access information for research or other purposes. To access information remotely, users can connect to a computer and access information wherever available, in cities, states, or global. In addition, work-at-home is a way a company allows their employees to stay at home and create a working environment there through the Internet. The files are shared via electronic mail to customers, or uploads and others. These files contain user authentication that was secured during transmission over the Internet. The authentication of files may require digital signature or others (Wikipedia b, n.d.).

The intranet is an Internet TCP/IP protocol that is privately owned and allows access only to its members, employees, etc. The intranet is secured by a firewall that denies access to an unauthorized user. Intranets also share information like the Internet, but to intended users. The HTTP, e-mail, FTP, or other is used for information access. With firewalls, user authentication, and organizational data and computing sources, workers share this information externally. Intranets provide tools and applications such as collaboration, sales, or project management and more to increase computing power.

Table 2.0 Intranet Benefits

Intranet Benefits
Increases workforce productivity
Time
Communication
Web publishing
Business operation and management

The intranet, as illustrated in Table 2.0, increases workforce production by allowing employees to find and view what to perform on a daily basis. This allows them to access information from anywhere, anytime, for fast and accurate processing. With time, companies make information resources accessible daily, instead of just e-mailing. Communication through an intranet uses tools within companies such as vertical and horizontal ones. Web publishing allows companies with the right tools to publish their information via hypermedia. In business operations and management, an intranet provides a way to develop and deploy applications that would support their business operations, or in decision-making. The disadvantage of using an intranet is that the resources provision might be lost. The information may not be secure enough to prevent unauthorized users from entering the system, or it being abused by outsiders or internally. The information overload is another concern (Wikipedia c, n.d.).

An extranet is a private network mostly used by its members, and also shared by outside parties for business or operations with the uses of Internet protocol. The business information or operations are shared between suppliers, customers, partners, etc. In other words, an extranet is thought of as extending outside uses, another way of doing business (Bury, 2005).

The use of extranets by organizations as follows:

➢to share information with the use of electronic data interchange (EDI)

➢to share product information with wholesalers

➢to share developmental processes with other companies

➢to develop and train with other companies

➢to provide services such as online banking for others

➢to share news among partner organizations

An extranet provides the ability for companies to share information with the use of virtual access. When an extranet is implemented, the process is known as virtual private network (VPN). The implementation of a private network requires that the network lines or phone lines be operated and owned by that particular company. Any messages sent through these lines are usually encrypted. Public Internet service providers are used to provide such services (Satzinger et al., 2004).

CHAPTER 4

THE APPLICATION

ARCHITECTURE

The system design activities carried by the people and hardware?

Application architecture design is the creation of business-specific. System designers must ensure that the structure design and functions are appropriate for a particular organization (Simpson, 2004). The application architecture handles the data distribution, processing, interfacing, and between-network locations. This process design is done via a distributed computing environment. An application architecture design is determined by organizational need. When developing enterprise application architecture, the process must define an enterprise-wide system. The applications are usually separate from the development itself (Whitten et al., 1998).

In order to maintain ongoing competition within information technology, many organizations use the Web systems, outsource, or software packages. Keeping such trends, the software architecture provides a way of combining various tools or services that support them. The sharing of architecture makes it possible to clarify in terms of whether an in-house or off-the-shelf or mix would be best. The use of shared architecture decreases the developmental cost. In turn, companies would be able to maintain coding, reduce production, document, train, and market the products (Dikel, M.D., D. Kane, & R.J. Wilson, 2001).

An application design again depends on requirement specification. Deploying a single personal computer system that includes video terminals requires a less complicated application. Employing a complicated distributing environment, hardware, or network would need complicated application architecture to implement such a system. We will discuss client server computing, multi-tier, middleware, Internet, and Web architecture as well as the designing bottlenecks (Satzinger et al., 2004).

CLIENT-SERVER ARCHITECTURE

The client-server architecture is responsible for the process of application that separates the two programs into client and server. The client computer manages the user interface information presentation. The database server stores data and/or processes queries. Figure 4.1 illustrates the client-server architecture processes. With client/server, database recover, secure, or accesses data done with central server. The user's personal computer runs through local area network (LAN). The database management system (DBMS), known as a database engine, is based for client-server. Moreover, with a server, all data requested must be similar to the client workstations via network. The client, on the other hand, focuses on user interface or manipulating of information.

For a centralized database system within a mainframe, any client/server application built must not be the same, since each client is requesting processes through the use of an application system. The interaction between user and devices such as printer, keyboard, screen, or more, are all handled by application. The server/client engine is responsible for accesses or controls. A client requests processes from the database engine. In addition, the central computer is responsible for managing or executing the mainframe information system (Jeffery, A.H., F.J. George, & S.J. Valacich, 1998).

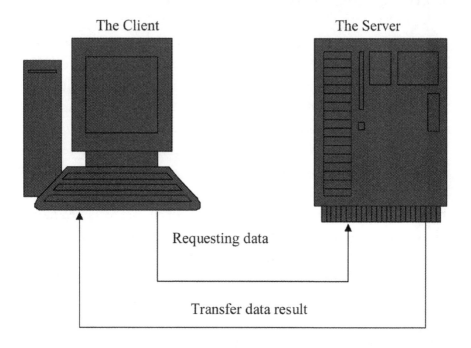

Figure 4.0. Client-server architecture

When designing the application for client/server, all specification requirements must be identified. This control process decompositions such as security, authorization, credit authorization or schedules are identified for accessing information, updating. The client/server application runs on almost all hardware systems, which are usually a

distributed computing environment. Another designing issue measured is client /server communication through Internet protocols. The physical network consists of a LAN or WAN, which runs over transmission communication protocol and Internet protocol (TCP/IP) for serving its users. All the requests, transfers of data, or services, language used, or protocols must be well-defined. Languages such as structured query language (SQL), using open database connectivity (ODBC) database are used within DBMS. Any required formation, segment of request, or response should be specified. For example, the client/server application design, especially credit authorization for an outside company, must be thoroughly stated. The benefit for employing client/server is that it is flexible within a distributed environment as well as computer networking.

Table 3.0 Network Benefits

Network benefits
Flexible Location
Scalable
Maintainable

Flexible location in Table 3.0 means networking provides movement of activities that changes the location or size system. The scaling is the processes that modify the system by increasing its computing capabilities, maintaining the system with updates that might be affected by the internal system, no change among others, such as credit card information. The client and server disadvantages are performing, securing, or being reliable, since communicating via network creates some communication issues such as those just measured. Moreover, any application that is central to one computer system doesn't require IP, as long as the system provides security, reliability, and/or runs efficiently. Employing centralized client/server architecture, many companies found it desirable due to its flexibility (Satzinger et al., 2004). In the next section, we discuss the three-layer client/server architecture and the underlying issues of the system, the processing of information through a network of computers among the three layers.

Three-Layer Client-Server Architecture

The client and server architecture is distributed to provide the two separate programs, the client or server-computing environment, to form three distinct applications. The evolving client/server architecture, the three-layer client-server consists of data management, presentation, and analysis combined into one system application to the creation of client or server (Jeffery et al., 1998). In other words, building a workable "heterogeneous" distributing system, an application architecture that is employed (Loosley et al., 1998).

The three layers employed within this architecture are:
> data layer is responsible for storing information into a distributed database system
> business logic layer is responsible for implementing or the process of data
> view layer is the process that allows users to view or process data

Figure 5.0, The Three-Layer Client-Server, shows the three layers, when a user, the client requests information, the business/client enables the data/client layer to interact (Satzinger et al., 2004).

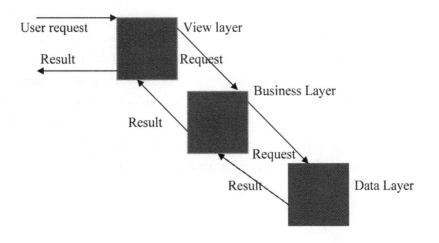

Figure 5.0 The Three-Layer Client-Server

The data layer is the storage of all data into distributed databases. Developing such layers requires a database management system (DBMS) as SQL server, Access, Oracles, MySql, or files to allow request/response from data. With SQL Server or Oracle, queries are rather simple, because languages are written very easy to do. This, in turn, reduces the complexity of the data layer. In addition, XML, CSV, or others make the formatting of the information easy. With the view layer, the layer provides user interfaces interacting with the system. The business layer transforms data requested and results to the end user. Business layer data transformation is the creation of business process. Although this layer requires no HTML, SQL, etc., it is important for designers to understand object-oriented programming (OOP) (Chartier, 2001), providing request/results.

When designing a communication within layers, for WAN network communication, tiers must be divided to reduce network traffic. Reducing the number of layers among a high-speed network could provide a fast and easy connection. With a slow network, some system designs are combined to increase communication or user interface

(Loosley et al., 1998). The advantages of employing three-layer client and server architecture are that programs are designed to fit a company's requirements. Customers access data through the data layer client via a database. The application flexibility allows interfacing among users.

We will discuss the trade-offs (see Appendix C) among layers that best describe a particular communication network. Tiers are required to be flexible, independent, perform, available, less expensive, upgradeable, manageable, and/or provide a secured system (Umar, 1997).

MIDDLEWARE

Middleware distributes computing resources at many areas anytime, anywhere around the globe. Middleware is defined as a set of applications that enables business services and users to interact with others over a network. Its enables technology for distributed enterprises is increasing that combine the process of Web, object-oriented, or client and server delivering good services. Middleware packages are also available in many software vendors that provide distributed comp-soft. Installing middleware that does not deliver could create a problem for global information systems. Middleware components are critical to many companies, since high-level middleware applications development needs to be understood before implementing it.

The middleware functions layer makes it possible to develop and deploy distributed applications, since layers are within programs via APIs. For instance, the layers that are used in application programs include:

Table 4.0 Middleware Layering

Middleware Layers	Their responsibilities
Network programs	For TCP/IP
Prime services	Terminal emulators and file-transfer
Client-server software	Information exchange
Distributed data-management software	Remotely accessing databases
Distributed transaction-management software	Guarantees transactions over systems
Distributed-object software	Allow access and invocation of objects over systems
World Wide Web	Supports applications across Internet
Special software	Mobile computing, distributed multimedia, groupware, and legacy integrated system

System designers must well define the type or types of layers to be used to implement middleware. For instance, in order for users to interact, DBMs provide protocols that make it possible, including ODBC or SQL. DBMS Software vendors provide such software or others such as third-party. The third-party software vendors include software for credit bureaus or electronic purchases or bids. In addition, protocols are used for industry-specific, including banks or healthcare (Satzinger et al., 2004). The complexity of object orientation that distributes over layers and hardware depends on ORB distributed object interface that is CORBA based. Non-object-oriented distributed software depends on specific middleware, such as DCE and/or Microsoft COM+. Web-based programs depend on Web-oriented, Microsoft .NET and/or Sun J2EE.

The Internet and Web-based Application Architecture

When developing a Web-based application that improves time or cost, and interacts with clients, suppliers, or business partners, it is important. The Internet has a different direction on how we communicate or do business. This provides the dissemination of information (strategies n.d.). The Web-based applications such as Web site, intranet, extranet, management, and personnel. The increase in designing such applications is rapid.

The Web services through a server rely on a server that executes on a dedicated computer or multi-computer. The programs that are responsible for sending and requesting information from a server using one or more Web protocols are called clients. Some webs are capable of embedding applications that are Web-like. The Internet and Web-based provides some alternating implementation for an information system. The most important aspects of Internet alternatives are being flexible. The use of the Internet has increased the implementation of applications, in turn, increasing application access and reducing client software installation. This software is available for update via Web server. Specifying which application to use over the Web, intranet, or extranet has some advantages that are illustrated in Table 5.0.

Table 5.0 Internet and Web-based benefits

Internet and Web-based benefits
Access
Reduced communication cost
Standards are widely implemented

With accessible Web browsers and Internet, as shown in Table 5.0, the application enables interactive Web sites to access users such as customers, suppliers, or employees other than office-based. Communication cost reduction the cost of WAN that enables the

Internet backbone does not cost anything to users. Although LAN is paid for by their users per month, the cost is reduced and companies can save money using a WAN. The standards are widely implemented, such as client server, or applications are available at a reduced price.

Table 6.0 Internet and Web-based negativities

Internet and Web-based negativitie
Security problem
Reliable
Throughput
Volatile standard

The disadvantages of using Internet and Web-based applications are shown in Table 6.0. Security is of concern when connecting networks and using the Internet, and the Web is subject to computer intruders. The network reliability for information delivery is not always guaranteed that it will reach its destination. The throughput, the transportation of data of home-based users' 56k modem. When LAN and WAN traffic exceeds its load, the networks become slow in responding, delaying access to many users.

With volatile standards, the Web applications design changes are increasing due to increasing functional compatibilities.

The Web-based and Internet architecture design issues are the same as client/server. The client and server design is subject to distributed computing and hardware connection to the right network, middleware, or protocols. With Web-based, choosing middleware or protocols limits in terms others (Satzinger et al., 2004). In chapter 5, we will illustrate the network design that connects information technology.

CHAPTER 5

DESIGNING THE NETWORK

The various part systems used to communicating among each other all over the organization?

When designing network locations, the communication requirements resources are thought of as operation locations and the various locations need to communicate with each other. A specific technology requires an individual location. Most importantly, systems that connect globally and integrate with other systems such as customers, suppliers, or others, are mission critical. The systems analyst must understand how the communication requirements that are usually distributing or sharing information within various locations would present the network (Whitten et al., 1998).

Many companies now use networks almost anywhere around the globe. In turn, increases need to design networks to stay competitive. The design and network plans are a crucial part of multi-layering (Satzinger et al., 2004). The issues that must be addressed when designing a network are:

> ➤ Network integration activities for the new system and between network infrastructures that already exist.
> ➤ Description of network processes and connections with different system locations.
> ➤ Describing communication protocols and middleware layers connections.
> ➤ The network capacity that satisfies the system.

NETWORK INTEGRATION

When networks interconnect with each other, they must be supported by a variety of applications. The integration of the new systems infrastructure must incorporate with the current system without problems (Satzinger et al., 2004). The applications software used is usually purchased, in-house, or obtained from a consulting firm. The consultation firm determines how the new system would work along with the current system, which provides the required connections and the configuration of firewalls.

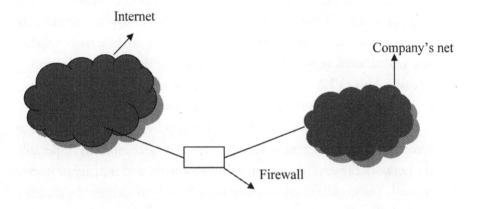

Figure 6.0 Firewall connects company's network

A secured firewall for connecting among a company network is very important. In other words, this firewall acts as a safeguard to the company's information systems (Comer, 2001). The most important part of employing a firewall is securing:

➢All traffic that enters the organizational network
➢All traffic that leaves the company's network
➢And rejecting all traffic that is inappropriate
➢Preventing security attacks

The firewall reduces security costs, is able to prevent hackers, and small packages are restricted by management from entering the network. Companies save costs by installing firewalls.

The most fundamental part of network design is making the network successfully implemented. The IP address planning address the logical design which will support the new network. The tools used to implement IP address include variable-length mask and routing. It is critical to employ the right route protocols, since the route protocols must support organizational standards. The design of a wide area network (WAN) is to examine the different technology and options available, especially when dealing with synchronous relays, ATMs, DSL, or others. With local area network (LAN), designing the network associates like those of campus LAN. The use of Ethernet switches across a network is beneficial to the success of the system. Motivating virtual LANs (VLAN), it is important to know the underlying issues before implementing the system (Searchnetworking a, n.d.).

However, configuring a network that requires too many changes to accommodate the current system can create some complexity; especially the network capacity, communication protocols, and security protocols control. The network management must be able to identify the capacity needed. In addition, the current network must be understood, its operation and other applications. The systems analyst must be able to gather enough information about the system's implementation (Satzinger et al., 2004).

NETWORK DESCRIPTION

The information needed to describe the structure in terms of user location, processes, and data must be clearly identified. The processes of distributing computers, applications, or databases are needed for design decision-making. In addition, the capacity between user and location must be defined. The systems analysts usually draw conclusions based on the information that they gather during the analysis stage. This, in turn, enables them to make a design decision whether to implement the system.

The location for data is helpful, such as designing and integrating the network, designing the application architecture, or designing and integrating the database for the recommended system. The communication locations can either be offices, warehouses, or manufacturing facilities, customers, suppliers, employees, hotel/rooms, and autos for user access.

After the locations have been defined, the network design processing is expanded into process locations, communication protocols, middleware, or the capacity that will be used to communicate. The network description example shown in Figure 7.0 provides an overview of an application-specific. This demonstrates application layers over location-distribution and user workstations. The combination of applications servers and computer systems assumed location and network organization (Satzinger et al., 2004).

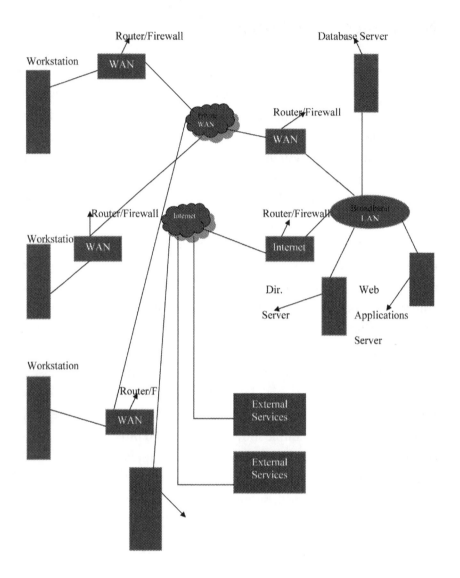

Figure 7.0 Network Demo

The figure above shows server locations, application servers into distributing area to increase systems performance. Even though the distributed servers might distribute to many locations that could create traffic problems, the system designers must be able to specify the locations, servers, and applications to be used by a specific company.

Communication Protocols and Middleware

The distributed computing that inter-operates, poses some issues existing within information distribution across networks. Middleware is the implementation of client/server. The communication processing application for more than two that runs across a variety of computer communication channels must be accomplished. (See Appendix D Protocol Communication Procedures.)

Moreover, network communications for middleware, such as remote procedure call (RPC) and network protocols such as TCP/IP, Ethernet, ISDN, etc. Designing communications distributed applications is mission critical. Communication with more than one program ensures inter-portability. Client and server provide communication directly and synchronously. With the different forms of communication available, organizations can employ what is best for them. Some types of communications are:

- ➢Synchronous or asynchronous
- ➢Connection-oriented
- ➢Direct
- ➢Client/server and roles
- ➢Partner and connection
- ➢Number of partners

Synchronous communication is a sending and waiting procedure for request/response. With asynchronous communications, the process of establishing a communication is through receiving and processing. The RPC is an example that works well with synchronous or asynchronous. A typical figure in 8.0 illustrates how synchronous or asynchronous works.

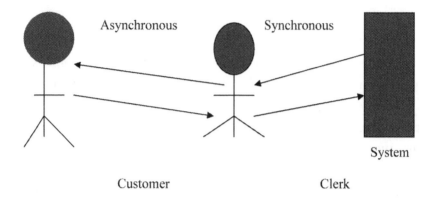

Figure 8.0 Synchronous or asynchronous

The figure above shows the customer communicating with the clerk, while using the computer system. With connection-oriented (see figure 9.0), application protocol is the process of connecting, disconnecting, and exchanging information across. Many varieties of middleware are implemented connection-oriented for being reliable.

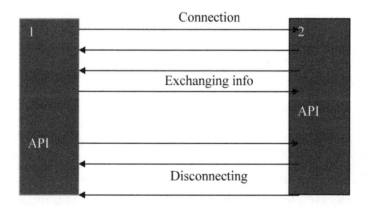

Figure 9.0 Connect-oriented

When directing communication, the middleware process is responsible for such communication and sends it to its destination. Client and server application, on the other hand, can be hybrid. Such as:

> ➢Client and server, the client's role is to request; the server's to respond
> ➢Peer-to-peer, the respond/request don't have to be the same

The availability of a partner requires some communication availabilities, and connection can be either connectionless or connection-oriented. The number of partners with middleware applications can be more than one partner communicating with each other. The availability of middleware to communicate implementation is crucial in terms of applications. The amount of capacity for any server to handle is limited. Workstations send information over and over, making the server vulnerable, causing a network delay (Loosley et al., 1998).

The specification of protocol and middleware required for a private WAN should be able to work well with the database and servers. A failed WAN means the private network would not function properly. The firewall ensures that all workstations communicate, all servers or outside services are protected (Satzinger et al., 2004).

NETWORK CAPACITY

Planning for network capacity for developing LAN, WAN, and Internet requires that all the necessary information needs to be evaluated in order to fulfill the network. The proposed new network would depend on how much it can handle in terms of functional capacity. A new application for a new network must be able to outperform the current system, to allow additional increases in capacity (NRC n.d.). The advantages for network planning are:

> ➢ It takes less time for full deployment
> ➢ The current system is evaluated toward the proposed system
> ➢ The implementation of a new application is specified
> ➢ The quality of service is improved
> ➢ The network is improved
> ➢ Delaying services to allow improvement

Moreover, network connectivity is specific dependent to the servers; an overloaded network could slow the server. The elimination of a server from limiting the network function, a 10-Mbps Ethernet, 100-Mbp Ethernet, or FDDI is used to increase the server's performance. When connecting to the Internet, the type of bandwidth depends on the amount of data received and sent to other networks. Table 7.0 discusses the type of connection and the size of bandwidth required.

Table 7.0. The Types of Internet Connection

Connection	Bandwidth
Dedication connection PPP/ SLIP	Modem
56K	56,000 bits per second
ISDN	56,000 to 64,000 bits per second
T1	1,540,000 bits per second
Fraction T1	Can vary
T3	45,000,000 bits per second
ATM	155,000,000 bits per second

Connecting computers to a network, the modem or ISDN connection uses any data transmission rate, bits per second. The users and file support must be identified to know the bandwidth requirement for the Web server and others. Other services such as e-mail, news, audio, or video are determined by the types of bandwidth used.

When connecting routers to the Internet, a high-speed connection is needed to avoid disruptions between the computer and the Internet. The connection to a T1 requires 1.54 Mbps bandwidth, and any server that resides on an Ethernet LAN requires 10 Mbps of bandwidth. With T3, an Internet connection requires 45 Mbps bandwidth; the type of connection should be distributed data interface (FDDI).

With HTTP, compressing data and/or applications among browsers is quicker. A restricted network would require application compression using HTTP style. Employing HTTP compression can be expensive, especially with files, since they are not usually stored. It requires some recreation and other forms of compressions are minimal in terms of cost (Microsoft b, 2000).

The transfer of information to and from users and the amount of period required to reach its destination is sampled in Table 8.0. The

HTTP can transfer files or pages fast within seconds. The files received from outside sources may take a few more seconds.

Table 8.0 Number of pages transfer

Type of connection	Number of pages transfer
Dedicated connection PPP/ SLIP	> .2 < = .6
56K	= .9
ISDN	= 1.7
T1	= 24
T3	= 710

In order to transmit the file between browsers, the number of users needed to connect and transfer data must be specific, as shown in Table 9.0.

Table 9.0 Number of users handled

Type of connection	Number of users
Dedication connection PPP/ SLIP	2 to 3
56K	10 to 20
ISDN	10 to 50
T1	100 to 500
T3	10,000 or more

CHAPTER 6

SUMMARY AND
CONCLUSION

INTRODUCTION

This study examines how systems design could help with optimizing scarce computing resources in applications or system performance constraints. Also, the hardware and software played an important role in determining the way in which an application performs, and the resources issues as well. With design activities, as measured earlier is the process that addressed the structuring, organizing, and describing in-depth of how the system would work into a different organizational setting (Satzinger et al., 2004). Even though some of the design detail sometimes did along during the systems analysis and the system activities.

The systems analyst must try to adapt to their preferences and user tools. Promoting a good integration between the ever-changing user's needs and information systems methods, we must develop a system that would ensure these changes (Whitten, & Bentley, 1998).

System design activities required during the design of a new system include designing and integrating network processes to specify communication activities for an organization, designing the application architecture, designing the user interface, designing and integrating the database, designing prototype details, and designing and integrating the system controls; in other words, the process of securing the system. in the next section, we will summarize the designs for a new system.

Summary

The architecture of the new system is drawn from the outputs design. The inputs design takes place during the analysis phase. The implementation of inputs, outputs, or systems design depends on the specific system. A different system requires different implementation. The design of application architectural could be broken in small parts to make the design process easier.

The deployment environment is the hardware, software, and the networks for the new system. These applications can distribute to a wide computing area in terms of client/server or three-layer. Designing the architectural requires the application be decomposed to the client, server, and/or layers that distribute the application via hardware. As a result, the protocols, middleware, and/or networks must be identified.

Designing and integrating network computers, we form a network to share or exchange information that integrates others. The most fundamental part of network design is making the network successfully implemented. The IP address planning addresses the logical design which will support the new network. Tools are used to implement IP address, such as variable-length mask and routing. It is critical to employ the right route protocol.

The networks used today include local area network (LAN), which provides one area, and wide area network (WAN), which provides service for more than one area. The applications make it possible to provide network services such as Internet protocol. Network capacity for developing LAN, WAN, and Internet require that all the necessary information needs to be evaluated in order to fulfill the network. The proposed new network would depend on how much it can handle in terms of functional capacity.

Advantages/Disadvantages

The system interfaces "bottlenecks" are usually not easy to recognize; it takes some time to know exactly what it going on with the system. The problems could result from inefficient processing that might sometimes be due to information overload. In order to get a better understanding of the interface scales is to minimize data load (CMS Watch, n.d.). When designing system interfaces, the designer needs to specify the types of output devices and transmission bandwidth that will be use for scalability, efficiency, flexibility, user-friendliness, and maintainability. This system requires a through technical background to design the interface system.

The advantages of database are scale, sharing data, balancing requirements, enforcing standards, controlling redundancy, data consistency, security, increased programmer productivity, and data independence. The economy of scale of one location with small amount and huge computer provides the scale. The sharing of data occurs in authorized users' environment that integrates information applications. The DBMS provides the location and accesses to satisfy the processes. Balance required conflict, the database administrator (DBA) is responsible for structuring the database for organizational benefits. Enforcing standards, the data names, usages, formats, or documentation are usually done by DBA. Control redundancy is a process that helps in eliminating the excess data in the database. Data consistency is present when the excess data has been removed from the database. Security is the definition of a process to eliminate unauthorized users from accessing the database. The increase in programmer productivity is due to just file accesses that allow them to do more. The use of fourth-generation languages increases their productivity. Data independence is a program that interacts within DBMS.

Disadvantages of database are size, complexity, cost, extra hardware, higher failure, and performance. Sizing the database is difficult to support complex functions. The complexity of database is that programmers must have some understanding of the DBMS features.

The cost of DBMS could be high due to functional requirements. Extra hardware, on the other hand, has to do with the size and complexity of DBMS. The high failure of the security, backup, and recovery could cost heavily, since the centralized single database means a failing DBMS would create a problem in the processing environment. The database performance—a single end-user processing is better and costs less to implement (Shelly et al., 1995).

The advantages of client/server are flexible location (see Table 3.0), network provides the activities that change the location or size system, providing scalable processes that modify the system by increasing its computing capabilities; maintaining the system with updates that might be affected by the internal system, no change among others, such as credit card information. The disadvantages are performing, securing, and/or reliability.

The advantages of the Internet and Web-based application are accessibility, as shown in Table 5.0, Web browsers and Internet. The application enables interactive Web sites to access users such as customers, suppliers, or employees other than office-based. The communication cost reduction is the cost of a WAN that enables the Internet backbone to not cost anything to users. Standards are widely implemented, such as client server or applications at reduced price.

Disadvantages of Internet and Web-based applications (see Table 6.0) are security is a concern when connecting networks and using Internet, and Web-based is subject to computer intruders. Network reliability for information delivery is not guaranteed destination. The throughput, the transportation of data of home-based users' 56k modem. LAN and WAN traffic exceeds its load, the network slows responding and delay access to users. Volatile standards Web applications design changes are increasing.

CONCLUSION

Systems design, the hardware and software are identified; the processes for the system and their interrelations are also described. The critical part of designing a good system is its quality, which is done before the building process begins (Martin, Brown, DeHayes, Hoffer, & Perkins, 2002).

During the deployment environment, the system required that the user locations, speed, or update, security, and transaction processing signify the environment. For instance, the level of transactions processed per day or more including credit-card payment-processing systems, would need a secured high-speed Internet, server, operating systems, and database management systems that would be compatible among each other. Hardware and systems software compatibility is based on how technology has changed. In other words, when Oracle and Sun systems merge, any systems changes occurring between the two would still integrate among each other. In addition, Microsoft operating and DBMS are integrated with processors such as Intel.

The most important thing to make sure about is that the hardware and software are compatible, to reduce high expenses. The system's external interfaces requirements bases on the outside processing, such as credit agencies, customers, suppliers, or government. The requirements of some software must be specified, as well as hardware, because a credit reporting agency might use a Web-based XML to service their customers, or CORBA-compliant. The applications interaction among interfaces must be compatible with system software.

The application architecture design, the information system must be designed to fit the user's preferences. (See chapter 4 about this topic.) Application architecture is application software that functions within a system network. During the design of application software, the user and database are designed as well. The design of the application must meet today's business requirement functionalities. Designing the software programs requires the use of computer tools to understand the various parts involved. System designers must ensure that the structure design and functions are appropriate for a particular organization (Simpson, 2004). The application architecture handles the data distribution, processing, interfacing, and between-network locations. Client-server architecture is responsible for the process of application that separates the two programs into client and server. The client computer manages the user interface information presentation. The database server stores data and/or process queries.

Designing a user interface is mission critical for the fact that users providing input to get a system output and learning process is very important (Wikipedia, n.d.). An information system depends on user interface, which defines the interaction between the user and computer. The user interface provides the graphics windows, dialog boxes, as well as a mouse to interact with. In addition, the interface is made up of sound, video, and voice, which might be different from one user to another. So designing a user interface is critical, something that systems analysts must thoroughly develop (Satzinger et al., 2004). The design of a user interface involves the design of input and output.

User interface, as stated earlier, requires human involvement at all time, since the interaction is based on the human and the computer to input data. The Web, on the other hand, the customer makes direct contact with the system by surfing through the Net. Developing interfaces for both the user and system requires different design, since the systems usually done separate with one another.

Database design is the process of designing the database structure that would house the data, instead of database management systems (DBMS). Good database design generates better data management and valued output. When a database design goes wrong, it is usually caused by redundancy or duplication of data. As a result of data redundancy, the erroneous data becomes hard to locate. For instance, social security numbers for customers, agent files, and invoices all store together makes it hard for that particular customer (Rob et al., 2004).

Though database is designed to handle the sharing data within applications and systems, but the complexity database has jet perfect. The redundant data is being reduced and controlled among databases.

The database benefit is to store formatting data, since it is database is separate in terms of information systems. The application programs specify which data should be in the end-user's areas. In a database, independent data must be carrying at all times for consistency. Aging reports and queries can be achieved by various well-designed databases. Designing a database is very expensive, investing in the technology required. The designing methodology and tooling for databases provides some significant improvement (Whitten et al., 1998).

Prototyping is a means of developing a quick, fast system so that users can provide some examination of the system. A complete verification of the system is done with a prototype. Further, the success of a prototype system depends on the architectural and being feasible. Programs that are not communicating with each other can cause a problem during testing. These programs can be formulated using a conventional or an object-oriented approach.

Prototype tools provide systems designers a way to develop a flexible and efficient system design. Such tools include Microsoft Visual Studio .NET, Oracle, as well as PowerBuilder for design satisfaction. The most fundamental aspect of developing a prototype is its speed and accurately defined user requirements. Constructing and modifying the system, the tools make it possible to do so without spending a lot of time.

A prototype that is powerful and flexible requires the development to be interactive. The process of developing a user interface prototype creates a way in which a user can interact within the system. All tools perform a different function from each other, like database management systems and Web site and so on. Choosing the right tools is critical in terms of suitable deployment, implementation, and interfaces.

The networks are built to allow many different accesses, from internal to external entities. The designing of these controls prevents many mistakes or hackers from accessing the system. The integrity controls make sure that any data coming in or out is valid. To maintain this validation, the Internet makes some walkthrough. Many companies are concerned about this issue of the Internet connectivity security, especially electronic market and sales.

The design of integrity controls of an information systems secured information within the system. Connecting on the Internet for companies that allow their workers, customers, and suppliers requires some security and integration of the system. Developing an application and database integration is crucial to the success of the company, known as integrity controls. When the operation system and network are controlled, this is known as security controls.

When designing security controls, the primary goal is to design a system that would prevent intruders from accessing the system; the same applies to integrity control, in maintaining a stable system where by protecting organizational a free of outside such as intruders, loaded information, worms, and viruses. Since many companies rely on the Web, any information transmitted is open to various attacks. Securing the operating system would mean to eliminate or control what could interrupt the systems environment.

The network locations, communication requirements resources are thought of as operation locations, and the various locations need to communicate with each other. A specific technology requires an individual location. Most importantly, systems that connect globally integrate with other systems, such as customers, suppliers, or others, and are mission critical. The systems analyst must understand how the communication requirements that is usually distributing or sharing of information within various locations that would present the network (Whitten et al., 1998).

The location of data is helpful, such as designing/integrating the network, designing the application architecture, or designing and integrating a database for the recommended system. The communication locations can either be offices, warehouses, or manufacturing facilities, customers, suppliers, employees, hotel rooms, and autos for user access. The system designers must be able to specify the locations, servers, and applications to be used by a specific company. Network communications for middleware include remote procedure call (RPC) and network protocols such as TCP/IP, Ethernet, ISDN, etc. Designing communications distributed applications is mission critical.

Communication with more than one program ensures inter-portability. Client and server provide communication directly and synchronously.

The availability of middleware for communication implementation is crucial in terms of applications. The amount of capacity any server has to handle is limited. Workstations send information over and over, making the server vulnerable, causing a network delay (Loosley et al., 1998).

Connecting routers to the Internet, a high-speed connection is needed to avoid disruptions between the computer and the Internet. The connection to a T1 requires 1.54 Mbps of bandwidth, and any server that resides on Ethernet LAN requires 10 Mbps of bandwidth. With T3, an Internet connection requires 45 Mbps of bandwidth; the type of connection should be distributed data interface (FDDI).

With HTTP, compressing data and/or application among browsers is quicker. A restricted network would require application compression using HTTP style. Employing HTTP compression can be expensive, especially with files, since they are not usually stored; it requires some recreation, and other forms of compression are minimal in terms of cost (Microsoft b, 2000).

Communicating via network creates some communication issues. An application that is central to one computer system doesn't require IP, as long as the system provides security, is reliable, and/or runs efficiently. Employing centralized client/server architecture, many companies found it desirable due to its flexibilities (Satzinger et al., 2004).

The Future Trends of Systems Design

The future trends in business or organizations have changed the way computing and others sources are done. Managements are faced with developing and deploying for the information system to stay current. In turn, the uses of new tools enable system designers to better upgrade in order to meet these changes. The end user's functional expectations must be increased as well.

The success of businesses or companies today is due to information systems and technologies. An information system interconnects information services, in other words is the component of people, data process, presenting data, and/or technology to support end users. A system is a collection of hardware, software, information, data, applications, communications, and/or people. The information technology enables the implementation of records, stores, or dissemination. The hardware is normally used for input processes.

The information system trends are critical to the success of organizations. The use of computer information systems is increasing every day to compute into the business world. But the increasing bottlenecks of the information system effectiveness is unanticipated. In turn, these issues could create a bridge for improvement for the organization. The most important thing that the information systems provided is the link to the Internet, which managers can use control their enterprise-wide or geo-location, and the government as well. Moreover, the recent computer and electronic data integration has created databases and policies between governments to speed development. This, in turn, provides a new way to do business and enable organizations to increase developmental processing.

The shift in information systems has increased the business functions instead of a single process. The rapid change in business processes is based on customer focus, which questions the current system's functionalities in order to satisfy such changes. The system designers or workers must be able to meet such requirements to satisfy organizational needs, ensuring that the information systems resources availability, and also the concerns of the system to be reliable and efficient enough to failures (e-zine articles, n.d.). The information system must be reliable and efficient to overcome interpretability among others; the emerging applications are available for purchase or in-house.

In addition, the architectural support of a wide range of implementation is needed. The application for a specific industry must support hardware. The Web-based, client model program for importing data from Web servers, data exporting and Web interface. When the speed of CPU chips increases, the Java and JavaScript code can provide a faster service. The Web has gained the popularity of buyers, sellers, or information resources seekers. XML or SOAP protocols enable the transportation of information requests.

The XML markup language standards is the process that defines the text and structural Web-based. The Internet provides a way to interconnect processes. The Web-based and XML extends the global information processes. Further, the use of the Web into intranet, in-house, private, which provide access to its intended users. The use of Web-based, JavaScript, and Java languages can enable the intranet to use applications that integrate many operating systems.

Networking trends go from shared media to switch, development of high-speed, or to TCP/IP standards. They usually share the bandwidth among networks. The Ethernet switches have increased the user computing speed as well as virtual LANs. A high-speed network uses Gigabit Ethernet or 10 Gigabit Ethernet for its backbones. Even though the network upgrades increase its processing speed, the system still poses some operation complexity. Creating and sharing of the HTML pages that organizations used to advertise intranet information. The corporate databases are usually used to extract data for publications.

APPENDICES

APPENDIX A:

SYSTEMS DESIGN SURVEY ASSESSMENT

The evaluation of the system design activities that is best describes the processes. The evaluation of this process will contain two graphs, one for systems output and the other for user interfaces, to see how likely the system acts. As measured in chapter 1, the overall rate of responders is $3/16 = .1875$ percent. Sixteen copies were distributed, and only three responded.

The ratings are based on a range from 0 being the lowest and 5 being the highest. Please circle the appropriate number.

System output	Low				Highest	
1. Accurate information.................0	1	2	3	4	5
2. Complete information.................0	1	2	3	4	5
3. User-friendly.............................0	1	2	3	4	5
4. On-time information..................0	1	2	3	4	5
User Interface						
5. Clear instructions......................0	1	2	3	4	5
6. Display help messages................0	1	2	3	4	5
7. User-friendly.............................0	1	2	3	4	5
8. Display appropriate options...........0	1	2	3	4	5
9. Display error messages................0	1	2	3	4	5
10. Prevent input errors.....................0	1	2	3	4	5

A-Graph: a. System Output

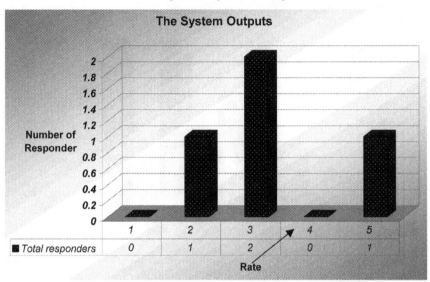

System output	Lowest				Highest
1. Accurate information....0	1	2	3	4	5
2. Complete information...0	1	2	3	4	5
3. User-friendly...............0	1	2	3	4	5
4. On-time information......0	1	2	3	4	5
Total responders	0	1	2	0	1

Graph A above illustrates how the system outputs behave; the number of rating is below average, which shows some problems with system outputs. The issues involved here include accurate information delivery, completeness of information, user-friendliness, and the information delivery time are inappropriate.

Graph-A: b. User Interface

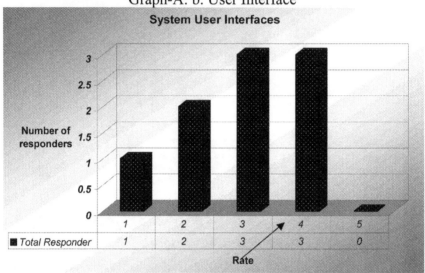

User Interface

		1	2	3	4	5
1. Clear instructions	0	1	2	3	4	5
2. Display help messages	0	1	2	3	4	5
3. User-friendly	0	1	2	3	4	5
4. Display appropriate options	0	1	2	3	4	5
5. Display error messages	0	1	2	3	4	5
6. Prevent input errors	0	1	2	3	4	5
Total Responders		1	2	3	3	0

The systems requirements assessment for the system output complexity as shown in Graph B above, rating for accuracy is mostly favored at a rate of three out of five. Two people responded the system output to be on the average. The information completeness, user-friendly, on-time information is either zero or one rating. Overall, both the system outputs and user interfaces need some improvement in those areas.

Appendix B:

Project Coordination

Coordinating a project for designing a system is critical, due to its many task requirements, since the design of the system would require in-depth monitoring or coordination. The business rules during design must be followed to avoid any project delay. When making decisions on a new system, the project team and user must have some understanding about the capabilities, modification, systems automation, and supporting the new system. The more design activities, the more issues to be fixed. These projects are sometimes broken into small projects. Project members are usually few in grouping to understand the divided projects.

The network, database, distribution, or communication present design issues that teams should beware of, since the projects are being sub-projects. Project coordination depends on the way the new system performs. Coordinating many sub-projects takes time and complication because team members are distributed in different areas.

Team Coordination

When coordinating a team, project managers are responsible for the scheduling of project activities and distributing them to team members. In addition, the project manager helps with tasks, which makes it difficult to handle in some cases.

Information Coordination

The coordination of information modules, data fields, classes, structures, forms, reports, methods, subroutines, or tables requires a lot of time. The tools available to handle such information include CASE tool to the recording or tracking of information. The best thing CASE tools deliver is being a centralized reposition. This is responsible for information reposition and configuration as well. Figure B illustrates the CASE tools performance.

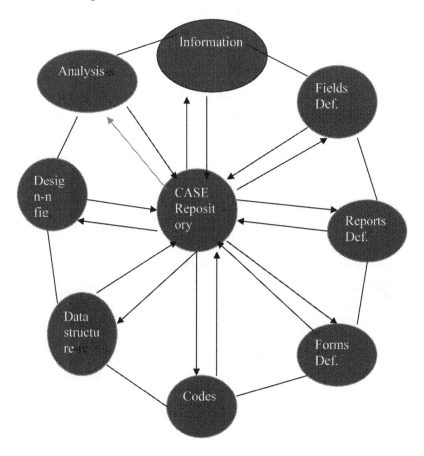

Figure-B CASE tools

The online collaboration tools are also available for coordinating a project. The team members can communicate with each other anywhere and anytime around the globe (Satzinger et al., 2004).

Appendix C:

The Three Tiers Tradeoffs

The three layers or mixed client and server shown in Table C provides some differences with each other in terms of implementations (Umar, 1997).

	Single tier	Two tiers	The Three tiers
Applications	Enterprise-wide OLTP	Support	Enterprise applications
Flex/growth	No	Yes	Yes
Independent user	No	Yes	Yes
Performing	Host traffic	Network traffic	More to choose
Available	No	Yes	Yes
Money	Less	Average	Expensive
Cost to upgrade	Expensive	Average	Less
Managing/ controlling	Excellent	Average	No
Securing controls	Yes	Yes	No

Table-C Tiers trade-offs

APPENDIX D:

APPLICATION COMMUNICATION PROCESSING

Table-D Application communication

Application Network

Send procedure		Data		Receive procedure

Transmitting area		
Application layer	Data	Application layer
Presentation layer	Data	Presentation layer
Session layer	Data	Session layer
Transport layer	Data	Transport layer
Data layer	Data	Data layer
Physical layer	Data	Physical layer

NETWORK PROTOCOLS

The table above illustrates how application communication processing is carried out. The communication activities occur in two or more places. The levels of communications are:

> Hardware or software provide communication links.
> The determination of content or the communication layers.
> The middleware to describe the distributed application that includes hardware or software.

BIBLIOGRAPHY

Bls.gov. n.d. *Computer Systems Design and Related Services.* Retrieved July 15, 2006, from http://www.bls.gov/oco/cg/cgs033. html.

Brown, A. S. *The Value Matrix Approach: Creating success by reaching your personal and business goals.* 2005. 2nd Edition.

Bury, C. 2005. *Extranet.* Retrieved August 28, 2006, from http:// www.searchsecurity.techtarget.com/sDefination/0,,sid14_ gci21089

Chartier, R. 2001. *Application Architecture: An N-Tier Approach.* Retrieved August 29, 2006, from http://www.internet.com/icom_ cgi/print.cgi?url=http://www.15.

CMS Watch. n.d. *Interface Scalability.* Retrieved August 13, 2006, from http//:www.cmswatch.com/feature/92.

Comer, E. D. *Computer Networks and Internets with Internet Applications.* (Upper Saddle River, N. J.: Prentice Hall, 2001) 3rd Edition.

Date, C. J. *An Introduction to Database Systems.* (Boston: Addison-Wesley, 2003) 8th Edition.

Dikel, M. D., D. Kane, & R. J. Wilson. *Software Architecture: Organizational Principles and Patterns.* (Upper Saddle River, N. J.: Prentice Hall, Inc., 2001.)

Elmasri, R. & S. Navathe. *Fundamntals of Database Systems.* (Reading, Mass.: Addison-Wesley, 2000) 3rd Edition.

ezinearticles, n.d. *Information System trends.* Retrieved September 7, 2006, from http://ezinearticles.com/?expert=Saleha_Abbas. http://www.selectbs.com/leraning/analysis-and-design.html

Jeffery, A. H., F. J. George, & S. J. Valacich. *Modern Systems Analysis and Design.* (Reading, Mass.: Addison-Wesley, 1998) 2nd Edition.

Jonker, D. (2005). *Choosing Application Architecture.* Retrieved August 8, 2006, from http://www.ftponline.com/ea/magazine/spring2005/features/djonker/

Lash, J. 2003. *Digital Web Magazine-Prototyping with Style.* Retrieved August 20, 2006, from http://www.digital-web.com/article/prototyping_with_style/.

Loosley, C. & F. Douglas. *High-Performance Client/Server: A Guide to Building And Managing Robust Distributed Systems.* (New York: Wiley Computer. 1998.)

Martin, W. E., C. V. Brown, D. W. DeHayes, J. A. Hoffer, & W. C. Perkins. *Management Information Technology.* (Upper Saddle River, N. J.: Prentice Hall, Inc., 2002) 4th Edition.

Meyer, M. & R. Baber. *Computer in Your Future.* (Indianapolis: Macmillan, 1995) 2nd Edition.

Microsoft b, 2000. *Capacity planning.* Retrieved September 3,

2006, from http://www.microsoft.com/windows2000/server/iis/ core/iiprft.

Microsoft. a, n.d. *User Interface design and development.* Retrieved August 9, 2006, from http://www.msndn.microsoft. com/library/en-us/dnanchor/html/anch_uidesi.

NCR, n.d. *Network capacity planning.* Retrieved September 5, 2006, from http://www.ncr.com/services/cons.

Rob, P. & C. Coronel. *Database Systems: Design, Implement, & Management.* (Boston: Thomson Learning, 2004) 6th Edition.

Rogers, R., H. Sharp, D. Benyon, S. Holland, & T. Carey. *Human-Computer Interaction.* (Reading, Mass.: Addison-Wesley, 1994.)

Satzinger, J. W., R. B. Jackson, & S. D. Burd. *Systems Analysis and Design in a changing world.* (Boston: Thomson Learning, 2004) 3rd Edition.

Searchnetworking n.d. *Guide to IP network design.* Retrieved September 4, 2006 from http://searchnetworking.techtarget.com/ generic/0,295582,sid7_gcil.

Selectbs. n.d. *Analysis and design.* Retrieved July 17, 2006, from

Shelly, G. B., T. J. Cashman, J. Adamski, & J. J. Adamski. *Systems Analysis and Design.* (Danvers, Mass.: International Thomson, 1995) 2nd Edition.

Simpson, n.ln., 2004. *Importance of Application Architecture.* Retrieved August 29, 2006 from http://dev2dev.bea.com/pub/

a2004/01/Simpson.html.

Strategies n.d. *Web-based Application Development.* Retrieved

September 2, 2006 from http://www.strategies.co.uk/services/

Web-based-applications

Torres, M. J., and P. Sideris. 2005. *Surviving PC Disasters,*

Mishaps, and Blunders. (Scottsdale, Ariz.: Paraglyph Press.)

Umar, A. *Client Server Computing.* (Upper Saddle River, N. J.:

Prentice Hall Inc., 1997) 4th Edition.

Webstyleguide, n.d. *Interface Design: User-centered design.*

Retrieved August 21, 2006, from http://www.Webstyleguide.

com/interface/user-centered.html.

Whitten, J. L. & L. D. Bentley. *Systems Analysis and Design*

Methods. (Boston: Irwin McGraw-Hill, 1998) 4th Edition.

Wikipedia c, n.d. *Internet.* Retrieved August 28, 2006 from http://

wikipedia.org/wiki/Intranet.

Wikipedia. a., n.d. *User Interface.* Retrieved August 9, 2006 from

http://wikipedia.org/wiki/User_interface.

Wikipedia. b, n.d. *Internet.* Retrieved August 28, 2006 from http://

wikipedia.org/wiki/Internet.